SURVIVAL CHALLENGE

HUNGRY!

Could YOU find food in the world's wildest places?

STEPHANIE TURNBULL

A⁺

Smart Apple Media

Published by Smart Apple Media,
an imprint of Black Rabbit Books
P.O. Box 3263, Mankato, Minnesota, 56002
www.blackrabbitbooks.com

Designed and illustrated by Guy Callaby
Edited by Mary-Jane Wilkins

Cataloging-in-Publication Data is available from the Library of Congress

ISBN 978-1-62588-215-8

Photo acknowledgements
t = top; c = center; b = bottom; r = right; l = left
folio image Thinkstock; 2t Tamara Kulikova, b Zhukov Oleg; 3 Kondor83;
4 Borya Galperin; 5 lzf, inset Olga Danylenko; 6tr LeonP, cr ronstik,
c monticello, bl Laborant, br anaken2012; 7t Dragon Images, c Krzysztof
Wiktor; 8t Jacqui Martin, c AndyTu, b Sergeysolar/all Shutterstock;
9 EuToch/Thinkstock; 10l ChaiyonS021, c Panom, r Oleg Znamenskiy,
b Andriy Markov; 11 picturepartners; 12t Ainars Aunins, cl Lumir Jurka
Lumis, c Dario Sabljak; 14 Marek Velechovsky; 15 Dr. Morley Read;
16 Jovana Milanko; 17 Peter Zachar/all Shutterstock; 18l Heinrich van
den Berg/Thinkstock, r Pim Leijen/Shutterstock; 20 CandyBox Images/
Thinkstock; 23 Fotografiche/Shutterstock
Cover t Medioimages/Thinkstock, b AleksandrN/Shutterstock

Printed in China

DAD0056
032014
9 8 7 6 5 4 3 2 1

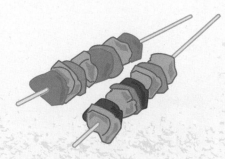

CONTENTS

Imagine you're an intrepid explorer trekking through deep jungle, dusty desert, wild woodland or icy Arctic wastes.

Things aren't going well. You're lost and confused, and the terrain is tougher than you expected. It may be days or even weeks before you reach civilization.

Dizzy and weak, you stop to munch an energy bar, then realize with a shock that it was your last one. Your stomach growls and the horrible truth sinks in—you could die out here in the wild.

Your challenge is to find food —fast. Can you do it?

You're going to need plenty of energy for climbing treacherous mountain ridges or hacking a path through dense undergrowth.

THINK SMART

You can survive for about a week without food (as long as you have something to drink), but you'll grow weaker every day. The weaker you are, the less able you are to hike, put up your tent or even think clearly.

RATION FOOD

First, check your backpack. Is there really nothing to eat? If you find something, don't wolf it down—have a little and save the rest. Eat things that will rot, such as apples, before things that won't, such as chocolate.

You should have packed energy-rich foods such as chocolate, dried noodles, nuts, seeds and dried fruit. A camping stove is a good idea too.

SAVE WATER

Without fluids you might die within three or four days, so look after your water supply. Don't spill a drop! Take small sips through the day rather than gulping it down.

If you're short of water, too, then you need another book in the series: **Survival Challenge: Thirsty!**

↥ *The more you sweat, the more water you need. Rest when it's hot.*

↩ *Even the most arid deserts contain food—if you know where to look for it.*

USE THE LAND

So you don't have so much as a candy bar. Don't panic! The land around you is full of food, and this book will tell you how to find it. But don't be greedy—take only as much as you need, then concentrate on getting home. And next time, plan your trip better!

*Ferdinand Magellan led an expedition across the Pacific Ocean in 1519. It took far longer than planned and soon all the food had rotted. Everyone got a painful disease called **scurvy**. They had to eat rats, sawdust, and old biscuits crawling with grubs. They even tried leather but it was too tough to chew. After 98 days they finally reached land.*

REAL LIFE SURVIVAL

7

PICK A PLANT

There are **edible** plants in wild places all over the world—and many of them are very good for you. Just don't pick all the plants from one area as they may then die out.

↻ Many ordinary weeds, such as nettles and dandelions, are full of **vitamins** and **minerals**. Boil them (see page 20) or eat dandelions raw.

IN THE ARCTIC
Think there's no food in the Arctic? Think again. Many mosses and **lichens** are edible but bitter. In spring, look for shrubs called Arctic willows. Pick new stems, strip off the bark and eat the tender shoot inside.

↑ Reindeer moss is crunchy and acidic, which may upset your stomach if you eat too much. Crush it and add to boiling water to make tea.

8

DESERT PLANTS

Don't despair if you're in the desert. Can you see a prickly pear cactus? Carefully saw off a thick pad with a knife, cut off the thorny needles and grill it over a fire. It's chewy and tastes a bit like green beans.

↻ *Wear gloves to protect your hands and be careful with sharp knives.*

Prickly pear cactus

Irish moss

SEAWEED SNACKS

Seaweed may look slimy, but it's packed with vitamins, minerals, and **protein**. Rinse it, boil it to a pulp, then eat it hot or cold. It lasts for days without rotting.

Sea lettuce

Bladderwrack

In 2012 an elderly woman named Tang Surong slipped into a deep ditch in a remote part of Leshan, China, and was stuck there for seven days before anyone heard her cries for help. She survived by drinking rainwater and eating handfuls of grass.

REAL LIFE SURVIVAL

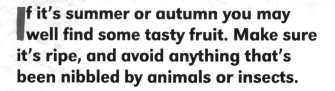

FIND FRUITS AND ROOTS

If it's summer or autumn you may well find some tasty fruit. Make sure it's ripe, and avoid anything that's been nibbled by animals or insects.

JUNGLE FRUITS

Finding fruit shouldn't be a problem in the jungle. More than 3,000 types of fruit grow in rainforest areas. Try bananas, coconuts, mangoes, papayas, and wild figs.

↻ From left to right: coconuts, bananas, papayas.

CHOCOLATE TREATS

Desert fruits include prickly pears, dates, and wild **gourds**. For a really sweet treat, find a carob tree, which looks like this.

➲ Low, bushy carob trees grow well in many hot, dry places.

10

Search the branches for long, dark brown seed pods. Pick the thickest ones you can find and avoid green pods (which aren't ripe). Break them open and pull out the seeds. The juicy, chewy pods taste just like chocolate!

GET DIGGING

Good things grow underground, too. **Tubers** such as potatoes and yams will give you lots of energy to keep going— but you must cook them first. Green potatoes are poisonous, so avoid them.

⋂ Carob pods keep well when dry, so fill your pockets with them to snack on later.

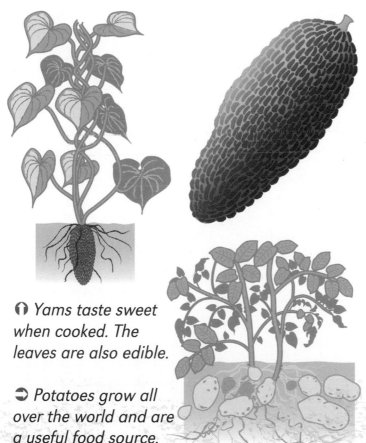

⋂ Yams taste sweet when cooked. The leaves are also edible.

⊃ Potatoes grow all over the world and are a useful food source.

REAL LIFE SURVIVAL

Nick Sales spent more than two terrible months drifting in the Pacific Ocean after his boat ran out of fuel. He survived by collecting coconuts floating in the ocean. He broke them open, drank the juice, ate the white, fleshy insides and even dried the shells and gnawed on them.

THINK BEFORE YOU EAT

Before you start snacking on the nearest berries, stop and think. Are you sure they're edible? Some plants can make you sick or even kill you, so don't take risks.

⮑ *Avoid red plants as many are poisonous, such as these bittersweet nightshade berries.*

MUSHROOMS

There are more than 1,000 edible types of fungi out there, but unfortunately there are also many poisonous ones—and it can be very hard to tell which is which. **There's only one solution: don't eat any mushrooms.**

⮐ *These mushrooms look similar, but only one is safe to eat. Do you know which? Find the answer on page 24.*

Twelve-year-old Lucy Adcock was cycling in woods one day and ate what she thought were two tasty field mushrooms. Next morning she began vomiting and realized that she had eaten highly poisonous death cap mushrooms! She was extremely lucky to recover in hospital.

REAL LIFE SURVIVAL

DO A PLANT TEST

Even edible plants can give you a rash or an upset stomach.
Always do this test first and only eat plants that pass every stage.

1. *Look closely at the plant. If it's old, wilted, nibbled or rotten, don't touch it.*

2. *Crush a leaf or stem. If the **sap** is milky, or smells like a sweet peach, it could be poisonous.*

3. *Rub the crushed plant on your arm and wait 15 minutes. If your skin comes out in a rash, the plant contains harmful chemicals.*

4. *Place a small piece on your lips. Does it sting, burn or itch? If not, place it on your tongue, chew it, and spit it out.*

5. *Feel OK? Chew another small piece and swallow it. If you feel ill, drink lots of water and try to make yourself vomit.*

6. *Wait six hours before you eat any more, to make sure you don't have a delayed reaction.*

TRY AN INSECT

Feel squeamish about crunching on a beetle or slurping up a worm? Get over it! Many insects are not only edible but also nutritious and could make the difference between life and death.

WHAT TO LOOK FOR

Edible insects include ants, termites, beetles and grasshoppers. Wash them and remove any wings or hairy, spiny legs, then roast or boil them (see page 20). You can also eat worms.

WHAT TO AVOID

Use your common sense when bug hunting! Brightly-colored or strong-smelling insects are probably warning you that they're poisonous. Ticks, flies, and mosquitoes can carry disease, so leave them alone.

WHERE TO LOOK

The only problem with insects is that you need a lot to make a meal. Look for insect homes so you can collect plenty at once. Carry a container to put them in.

Many insects live under stones.

Lift rotting wood to find insects living underneath.

Look out for ant hills like this.

⋒ This wolf spider could give you a nasty bite, so it's best to keep clear.

GREAT GRUBS

If you're in Australia, follow the example of **Aborigines** and use a sharp stick to dig fat, white witchetty grubs out of the ground. The grubs are soft and easy to chew, so you can try them raw or roast them like marshmallows.

Derek Mamoyac was climbing Mount Adams in Washington when he broke his ankle. Unable to walk, he spent days on the mountain. He ate a few berries but was still hungry, so he started eating ants, centipedes and even a large spider. The food kept him alive until rescuers found him.

REAL LIFE SURVIVAL

GO FISHING

Are you near a stream or river? If so, it will be full of fresh food—if you can catch it! Find some tips for preparing and cooking fish on page 20.

Always fish in clear, flowing water, not polluted or stagnant pools.

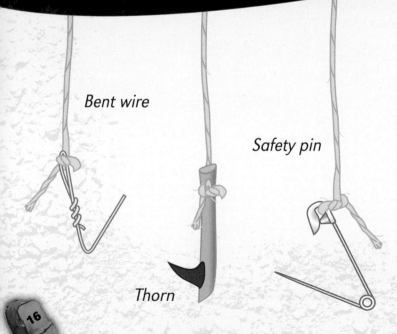

Bent wire

Safety pin

Thorn

FISHING TOOLS

You can wade into water and try to catch fish with your hands, but it's better to make a fishing line from string or a strip of cotton torn from a T-shirt. Tie on a thorn, safety pin or wire for a hook. Spear a worm, grub or insect on it as bait.

If you have a knife, make a spear by sharpening a stick or bamboo pole.

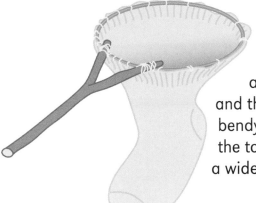

A sock makes a good fishing net. Tie it to a Y-shaped stick and thread wire or bendy twigs around the top to make a wide opening.

PICK YOUR SPOT

Choose a place where you can see fish. If it's hot, they're more likely to be in deep, cool water. If it's cold, look in shallow, warmer water. Now keep still and be patient—catching fish can take a long time!

Be cautious around water. Don't lose your footing!

REAL LIFE SURVIVAL

In 2010, three teenage boys, Samuel, Filo, and Edward, spent an incredible 50 days drifting in the South Pacific Ocean when their boat engine broke down. They survived by catching fish (which they ate raw) and also ate a bird that landed on the boat!

SEASIDE SNACKS

If you're near the sea, look for shellfish such as mussels, cockles, and whelks. They taste good steamed, boiled, or baked and eaten out of the shells. But eat them right away as they won't stay fresh for long.

GO HUNTING

Another option is to try hunting animals and cooking the meat. But be warned—hunting is hard without good tools and lots of skill. It's probably best to do this only if you're really desperate.

↻ *Some native peoples still learn to hunt in the wild.*

↪ *Catching a rabbit may be tricky. They move fast!*

COPY THE EXPERTS

Many people who live in wild places are skilled at hunting by following animal tracks. They also look for droppings, nests, burrows, and paths in vegetation that animals use regularly.

Rabbit

Front foot

Back foot

Grey squirrel

Front foot

Back foot

Deer

Front foot

Back foot

SLOWLY DOES IT

If you really want to catch a rabbit, deer or other animal, don't go crashing through the undergrowth—slow down, tread softly and scan the ground carefully. You may need to follow an animal's tracks for a long time before you see it.

HUNTING TOOLS

Some hunters use spears or bows and arrows. Others use a smooth, curved piece of wood called a throwing stick. Hold it at waist level, with the end in your palm...

... then throw it with a quick flick of the wrist, so it spins away and hits the animal.

In 1911, an explorer named Douglas Mawson ran out of food in Antarctica and had to kill and eat the dogs who pulled the sledges. He didn't know that dog livers contain a lot of vitamin A, which makes you sick if you eat too much. Desperately ill, Mawson reached safety just in time for doctors to save his life.

REAL LIFE SURVIVAL

GET COOKING

If you have a stove or can make a small fire, always cook the food you find in the wild. This kills **bacteria** and also provides comforting warmth.

HOW TO COOK

The easiest cooking method is to boil plants, insects or meat in a pot with water to make a soup or stew. You could also fry them in a pan or spear them on sticks to roast over a fire like kebabs. Hang pieces of fish on a log near the fire to cook.

Fish cooking on a log near fire

Meat and vegetables on sticks

OVEN COOKING

If you've got the time and energy, make a heated pit that works like an oven.

1. *Dig a hole about two feet (60 cm) deep. Heat big stones in a fire and roll them into the pit. Don't burn yourself!*

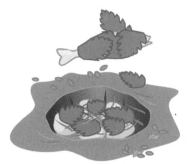

2. *Cover the stones with grass or edible leaves. Wrap food in more leaves and put it on top.*

3. *Fill the pit with leaves, grass and soil. Leave the food for a few hours to heat through, then dig it up.*

PREPARING FISH

What about fish bones? Here's how to get rid of them like an expert.

1. *Using a knife or sharp stone, slit the raw fish up toward the head, away from your hands.*

2. *Cut off the head just below the* **gills**.

3. *Open out the fish and pull the head and bones away in one piece.*

GLOSSARY

Aborigine
A member of a group of native Australian people. Many Aborigines are skilled hunters and trackers.

bacteria
Tiny, single-celled living things. Some bacteria are harmless, but others can cause diseases.

edible
Fit to be eaten; not poisonous.

gills
Openings on either side of a fish's head, used for breathing.

gourd
A large, tough-skinned fruit, similar to a pumpkin or squash.

lichen
A living thing, like a fungus, that grows on places such as tree trunks and bare ground. Lichens can be yellow, crusty patches or bushy growths.

minerals
Natural substances from the ground. Your body needs small amounts of certain minerals, such as iron and calcium, to work properly.

protein
A natural substance, found in foods such as meat, fish, eggs and nuts, that your body needs to stay strong.

sap
The liquid inside a plant stem.

scurvy
A disease caused by a lack of vitamin C. It can cause swollen gums and severe pain.

tuber
A thick underground stem or root.

vitamins
Natural substances that your body needs in small amounts to work properly. There are vitamins in all kinds of fresh foods.

www.thesurvivalexpert.co.uk/FoodandWaterCategory.html
All kinds of useful tips for finding food in the wild.

www.wildwoodsurvival.com/survival/food/index.html
What to eat, what to avoid, and how to cook the food you find.

www.backpacker.com/cooking-tips-and-tricks
Camp cooking tips and tricks.

INDEX

Answer to question on page 12

The mushroom on the right is an edible horse mushroom, while the one on the left is a destroying angel, one of the world's most poisonous mushrooms. Eating just half of one could kill you!